OF MIST AND STONE
A JOURNEY INTO THE MYSTERIOUS
ONENESS OF TWO ANCIENT WORLDS

John Two-Hawks

CSR Media

A Division of Circle Studios Records

Wopila / Buíochas mór (many thanks) to:

Johnice Cross – Proofing / Editing
Teresa Sullivan – Chapter Paintings
John Two-Hawks - Cover Photo – Galway, Ireland
Josh Kolb – Graphic Design
CSR Media – Concept / Layout

*Thank you to Bear McCreary, Mari Boine,
Brother Seamus, Celtic Woman and Enya.
Your music was the canvas upon
which this book was painted.*

Dedicated to all who hear the voice of the ancients
and seek to touch once again the sacred mystery

For John McGuire and Ann O'Farrell
What you lost in leaving I have found in returning

TABLE OF CONTENTS

Come away, O human child!
To the waters and the wild.
With a Faery hand in hand,
For the world's more full of weeping
than you can understand.

W.B. Yeats

~ Prologue ~

THE ONENESS OF
TWO WORLDS

As a person with Indigenous and Celtic lineage, both ancestral pathways have whispered to me of their secrets throughout my life. The ancient wisdom and knowledge which swirls in the mist of forgotten times has always beckoned my spirit. Those voices in the ether have drawn me to sacred, mystical places like Mato Tipi (a.k.a. 'Devil's Tower'), Brú na Bóinne (Newgrange), Mato He (Bear Butte), Knowth and Dowth, the vortexes of Sedona, and many other ancient sites throughout the Americas and Ireland. These places hold an energy that transfixes. They whisper of a people with access to spiritual power that we can only dream of today.

The Celts and the Indigenous peoples of the Americas are each unique unto themselves. They are not the same. And yet, I have come to see that there are mysterious ties that bind these two very distinct cultures in interesting ways. There are common threads of worldview, spirituality, racial oppression and social custom that are uncannily similar. I see those similarities as a window into a sacred knowledge the ancients collectively understood. Knowledge we in the modern world have lost touch with. Knowledge that could hold the secrets to how we save ourselves from our worst impulses and heal our planet. Though I am descended of both peoples, I wrote this book as an observer with the eyes to see into two worlds. My dear Métis friend and sister, Andrea Menard, once reflected that we of mixed ancestry are a bridge between cultures and that it is our job to translate from one to the other. This book is, in part, an attempt at that translation. One could persuasively argue that the Celts and Indigenous peoples are two of the most prolific human cultures on earth. Indigenous people occupy nearly every inhabitable land mass on the planet. And the descendants of the mighty Celts, who once dominated most of what is now Europe, now exist on virtually every continent. These two circular minded, spiritually powerful, earth-based peoples – though seemingly a world apart from one another – are mysteriously alike in the deeper, more mystical things. This speaks to more than an ancient spiritual connection between two cultures; it speaks to the common humanity in us all. And thus, there is a lesson to be learned from these profoundly illuminating alignments.

This book is less a historical account, and more an exploration of ancient mysteries and synchronicities. It is an invitation to enter into a deeper contemplation of the sacred connection we all share, by means of a fascinating journey into the oneness of two worlds.

1

SACRED CIRCLES

ANCIENT SECRETS
OF CYCLICAL POWER

I still remember the first powwow and wacipi (dance) I attended. The powerful, pulsating rhythm of the drum; the spiritual electricity of the voices singing old songs in unison; the dancers in their magnificent regalia stepping and whirling in perfect time to the beat of the drum; all of it – the sights, sounds and sensations – was life changing. The wacipi and powwow takes place in and around a circle and much of Native spiritual and cultural tradition also centers around the circle. Lakota holy man Hehaka Sapa (Black Elk) once said, *"Everything an Indian does is in a circle, and that is because the power of the world always works in circles, and everything tries to be round. The sky is round and I have heard the earth is round like a ball, and so are all the stars. The wind in its greatest power whirls. Birds make their nests in circles, for theirs is the same religion as ours. The sun comes forth and goes down again in a circle. The moon does the same and both are round. Even the seasons form a great circle in their changing, and always come back again to where they were. Our tipis were round like the nests of birds, and they were always set in a circle, the nation's hoop. The life of a man is a circle, from childhood to childhood. And so it is in all things where the sacred power moves."* Resting 9,642 feet atop Medicine Mountain in northern Wyoming lays an ancient wonder: A 1,500 year old circle made of stones. It is called the Medicine Wheel, and its features reveal a mysterious knowledge of the cosmos and lunar cycles. Versions of this stone wheel are seen in modern day Native cultural expressions from ceremonial practices

3

inipi - ceremony

to tee shirt designs. I have spent a lot of my life in and around sacred circles. I have been honored to sit at the sun dance drum as part of that ceremonial circle and join my voice in songs of prayer for those making an incredible sacrifice. The area where the dancers dance, the drum itself, and even the songs are all round. I have offered prayers and songs during the inipi ceremony, which takes place in a sweat lodge that is also in the shape of a circle and honors the four directions. I cannot tell you the number of times something unexplainable happens in that ceremony. As well as being centered on the tenets of the sacred hoop, the inipi involves the use of stones, which are heated to a glowing orange in the fire and brought into the lodge to receive the waters. So you can see the stones are still a part of the spiritual life of Native people. My wife and I also have a modern medicine wheel prayer garden on our land in the Ozark Mountains, where many offerings have been made by people from all over the world. Interestingly, the winds almost always whirl inside that wheel, even when the day is calm. And in the center is a mound of special stones from sacred sites around the globe. We have always endeavored to make this spiritual place available to everyone who has been there and touched its power. We do not feel ownership of it; we are merely its caretakers. Something powerful happens in these round places dedicated to ceremony. As with our Medicine Wheel garden, there is a swirling energy that cannot be explained.

Sedona

Years ago my wife and I traveled to Sedona. During our visit we were made aware of locations throughout the region called 'vortexes'. To put it plainly, they are places of spinning energy. If a tree sprouts up near the center of one of these whirling places, its growth becomes twisted, with the bark appearing almost like a rag being wrung out. We ventured out to explore one sunny afternoon and ended up in one of these areas. An amazing thing happened to me that day that I have never forgotten. I saw one of those twisted trees out on the red rocked hillside, and decided to go and have a closer look. Once I got to the tree, I paused and took a deep breath, making an honest effort to connect to whatever this energy was. You see, I am a bit of a pragmatist and a skeptic. I don't believe everything I hear. But I am also open to all possibilities. I wasn't sure what to think of all this 'vortex' stuff, but I was willing to give it a whirl (pun intended). So I took that breath and tried to tune in. After a few quiet moments I decided to reach out and touch the tree. The instant my hand made contact with it, a heart stopping thunderclap shook the ground and I nearly lost my balance I was so startled. I kept my hand on the tree, and felt a powerful feeling I still have a hard time putting to words. Suffice it to say I left Sedona a believer in the spinning places.

Throughout my life, I have had the honor and privilege to spend time with elders, holy men and teachers from many Indigenous cultures from every corner of the world. I once met two men of the San peoples of South Africa. One was a holy man and the other was a tracker. We communicated through a translator as they shared the story of how they had politely told their host that they just couldn't sleep inside a square house, separated from the earth, moon and stars. So it was arranged for them to sleep in a nearby park during their visit to the Indigenous music festival in Ohio at which we were both performing. That holy man gifted me with a handmade instrument that day called a mbira, a gift I still cherish. I have also had visits and interactions with the Sami people of Scandinavia. They too, use a circular, four directions symbol. Many years ago I was gifted a very special Sami 'Four Winds' hat and a Sami flag. Their flag features a circle, and I have seen this four winds wheel painted on their drums. One very special drum which was created in part by Sami influence is called The World Drum. That drum has the four directions circle painted on it, and it has traveled the world in the spirit of healing for mother earth and humankind. I have held and played that sacred drum, and I can tell you it has a power like no hand drum I have ever heard. As for the Native peoples of the Americas, I have visited with folks from tribal nations from sea to shining sea, and I have yet to encounter an Indigenous American culture that does not have a sacred circle as an integral part of their customs and spirituality. Thus you can see how deeply the circle has been integrated into Indigenous life around the globe from ancient times to the present.

∽

Speckled across the landscape of Ireland are stone circles, all many thousands of years old. I have stood in these places and felt their power. There is nothing quite like touching ancient energy. And yet, there is something about those stone circles that feels like the vortexes of Sedona; a spinning current that resonates with your spirit. On my most recent trip to Ireland, I visited a place near Galway called Brigit's Garden. It is a magical place, with a lovely shop and café. But the most wonderful things to see are outside. They have created numerous features which pay homage to the ancient Celts of long ago. There is a stone circle, a pathway with standing stones, a place that whispers of the Druids, a massive Fairy village, and many more enchanting things to see and experience. But it was the Fire Festivals wheel that made the deepest impression on me. I was astounded by its similarity to the Native American medicine wheel. The lessons imparted from the teachings of the Indigenous sacred hoop bear a remarkable resemblance to the seasonal fire festival wheel of the old Celts. Both pay homage to the seasons, the cardinal directions and the cycle of life. I have seen stone carvings of circles with four quadrants thousands of years old in Ireland that are nearly identical to the Native American medicine wheel. And the similarities don't stop there. Indigenous and Celtic peoples are both circular in their thinking and worldview. Each culture sees the pathway of life as a circle, with all things coming around again. Both are deeply connected to the natural world, with all its circular tendencies.

There is an inherent quality in Irish and Native people; they both see the roundness of the world. And I don't just mean the shape of the planet. Celtic and Indigenous people are indelibly tied to the earth. A tree is born of seed, soil, sun and water. It grows tall and grand, until the day it dies, falls and returns to the ground from which it came. It becomes the soil which nourishes the seed of a new tree which will spring forth with new life, thus continuing the ever spinning sacred cycle of life, living, death and rebirth. Native and Celtic people see this circle in all things. They interact with the world with this knowing; that all things come from and return to the sacred wheel of the natural order. This circular worldview shapes everything they see, do and feel. It is who they are. They are the sacred hoop. They are the circle, embodied in human form.

Brú na Bóinne, more popularly known as Newgrange, is a 5,200 year old circular Stone Age monument north of Dublin. Every year on the morning of the winter solstice, a ray of sunlight illuminates the inner chamber of this magnificent sacred site. I have been inside that chamber and experienced a

 - Dolmens

demonstration of that phenomenon. It was awe inspiring. Forming a ring around the base of this giant circular earthen structure are huge stones, many which are carved with megalithic symbols such as infinity spirals, chevron patterns and waves. Symbols which are almost identical to those that can be seen at ancient Native American sites. Then there are the dolmens. During my first visit to Ireland many years ago, we were driving somewhere near County Carlow in the South-East, when I looked out into a nearby field and saw it; three giant stones set up like a table. We pulled off and got out to pay a visit to what would turn out to be the *Brownshill Dolmen*, the largest dolmen in all of Ireland. I tell you, the huge top stone was much larger than a full size SUV. No one seems to really know what purpose the dolmens served the ancients that erected them, but they are prolific and can be seen all over Ireland. There was an informational plaque at the site that explained how those huge stones had come from a group of hills so far away you could barely see them on the horizon on a clear day. How the gigantic stones at these sites were moved and placed where they are remains a mystery that, to me, defies a physical explanation. It is widely accepted that the mysterious people who built Newgrange were very highly advanced. I believe it is possible, even likely, that the builders of Newgrange, Stonehenge, dolmens and the like had access to power and energy we cannot fathom today. Some studies have been done that suggest that the configuration of Stonehenge, in addition to being an astronomical computer of solar and lunar cycles, has something to do with sound waves, and that perhaps those sound waves played a role in the placement of those ancient stones. I don't have the answer. No one does. But simple common sense tells me that those giant stones weren't dragged and placed where they are by physical means alone. There is another explanation, one that requires an understanding of unseen power. Knowth and Dowth and other sites like them across Ireland are smaller, and not as well known as Newgrange, but bear the same features. Also, interestingly, Newgrange is aligned with the sun, but all the other sites are aligned with Newgrange. The circular design and astronomical alignment of these sacred places in Ireland whisper of an ancient, highly advanced people who knew the secret power of the circle. The Medicine Wheel in Wyoming speaks of the same. The ancient ancestors of modern day Native and Irish people had access to something we have lost today. Our search for matter-based answers to the mysteries and secrets of a people, whose power seems to have come from non-matter sources, have yielded little to no results. We have been looking in the wrong places.

When I first heard that drum at that wacipi all those years ago, I sensed its ancient power and electrifying energy. Those sounds penetrated something deep in my spirit, and awoke something in me that has never slept since. I believe that same power is what built Newgrange, Stonehenge and the Medicine Wheel. It is a circular energy. It is a sound wave. It is a song. It is breath. It is all things round. It is the sacred cycle of all life and the ancient secret of cyclical power. We must return to the stones. We must touch once again the mysteries of the ancients, and reconnect to the energy of the unseen and the power of the sacred circle.

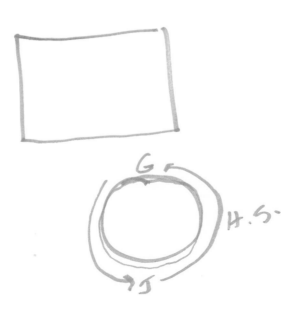

II

SACRED NUMBERS

SPIRITUAL MATHEMATICS

Did you know that a turtle has 13 spots on its shell, regardless of its age, size, or whether it is a box turtle, snapping turtle or sea turtle? And that the human body has 13 major joints and buffalo have 28 ribs? Are you aware that there are 13 lunar cycles in a year, and that each cycle is 28 days? That's right, the connection between the cosmos and the life on this planet is indelible, and the numbers that tie the web of life together are sacred. The people of ancient times knew the secrets that bind the stars and the earth together. They cast their gaze into the heavens for celestial guidance as to where they were on the ground and what direction to go. They looked upward for the answers to what lies below. The changing seasons and cycles of life are intricately connected to lunar and planetary rotations. The ancients not only understood this, they had tapped into and harnessed that unseen celestial power that draws an entire ocean away from the shore. That power is spinning energy, just like the vortexes of Sedona and the whirling winds in a sacred stone circle. All of it is rhythmic, pulsating, rotational and circular and moves in waves, much like music. A few years back, scientists used new technology to make audio recordings of a group of stars in deep space. By converting stellar oscillations into frequencies that can be heard by the human ear, the resonating of these ancient stars becomes audible. The resulting sound waves have an astounding musical quality. Music and sound holds great power. The human ear is capable of hearing a very impressive portion of the entire sound spectrum. And yet, there are sound frequencies in the universe that are beyond our ability to hear. This fact alone should pique our interest in unheard, unseen and unknown energy. The ancient ones of the Indigenous and Celtic worlds possessed a mysterious knowledge of these rotational, cyclical energies, and used sacred numbers to identify with them.

We begin with zero. The Mayan people conceived the numerical concept of zero over 1,000 years before it was introduced to Europe by Arabs in A.D. 800. Zero is the void, the nothingness. It is the acceptance of emptiness. It is that place devoid of light. It is the pivot point that binds the end with the beginning. Zero is that place where past, present and future are aligned. It is the sacred center, the place of mystery. As its very shape reveals, zero is the circle. It is completion. The cosmos itself is a zero-sum equation of celestial balance. That balance is what sustains all life on this planet, and it would not be possible without the zero; for the zero is the axis around which every numerical possibility and reality rotates. It is the center of the teeter totter, the hub of the wheel, and the point of the spinning top. Without zero, the suspended animation of all that is would cease to be. Zero is the mystery, the unknown and the essence of sacred energy. It is the evidence of things hoped for, and the substance of things not yet seen. Yes, zero is faith.

16

"Three hands before me." My dear friend, Brother Seamus Byrne from the Servants of Love Community in Wicklow, Ireland once told me an amazing story. He and I collaborated and released an album together back in 2002 called *Traditions – Indian & Celtic Music & Spirit*. Around that same time, Seamus had released a wonderful album called *Prayer Songs and Symphonic Poems*. The Irish have an old custom of creating personal prayer incantations and songs for spiritual protection. With that custom in mind, Seamus had decided to create his own personal protection song, and it ended up on his *Prayer Songs* album. The song is called *Three Hands*, and speaks of the protection and guidance of the holy trinity. It is a beautiful, soulful song, and Seamus had been performing it at concerts for quite some time when, one day he walked by a shop in Dublin that specialized in family crests. As Seamus explained it, he had never thought to look and see what the Byrne family crest was. The front window of the shop had a large alphabetized chart of family crests, so Seamus paused on the street and looked for his surname. When he saw it he said he nearly fell over. The Byrne family crest is a white shield with – you guessed it – three hands. I have never forgotten that story. The fact that Seamus was unaware of the significance of three hands to his ancestral Byrne family, and that somehow, from out of the ether, he chose to make his protection prayer song about three hands, speaks to a deeper knowing that we all have in us.

17

Something in Seamus' spiritual DNA whispered three hands into his consciousness, and he listened.

My McGuire and O'Farrell ancestors were forced to leave their beloved Ireland because of the Great Hunger (potato famine). I am certain that their longing for the homeland they would never return to is why I feel so strongly connected to that mystical emerald isle. My ancestors lost something in their leaving, which I am still trying to find in my returning. The circles of ancestral lives in our lineage whisper their stories and their longings to us in our dreams, reflections and aspirations. The past is never really gone, and the future is shaped by how we carry what once was into the present. In the Celtic world, past, present and future are three faces of one circular journey. They are not separate, but flow into one another. And it is the same for other Celtic concepts of three. There is probably no number more sacred to the Celts than the number three. It is the number of completion, being the sum of one and two. It is the number of wholeness, encompassing the beginning, middle and end. Woman and man together make a third life when a child is birthed. Three is the underworld, earth and heavens. It is land, sea and sky. It is above, below and here. The sacred number three is water, ice and mist; three versions of the same element, much like Father, Son and Holy Ghost. When Patrick brought Christian Catholicism to Ireland, it was surely the concept of the trinity that found alignment in the minds of the Celts who had such reverence for the triad. It was at least a part of the reason so many Celts became Christians. In the old Celtic world, the oak, ash and thorn were known as the fairy triad of trees, and where the three are found growing together, there the fairies live still. Three is also stability and strength. The Lakota tipi is built around a tripod; three poles tied together that hold up all the other poles and the cover. The old Lakota said that there was nothing stronger than the tripod. Lastly, much like the Celtic concept of above, below and here, Native ways teach about father sky, mother earth and the center as the final three of the sacred seven directions. The synchronicities abound. I do not know the origin of the three hands on the Byrne family crest, but I am quite certain the meaning is tied to the ancient Celtic knowledge of the power of the sacred number three.

Just as the number three is so important to the Celts, so the number four is to Indigenous peoples. The first ceremonial song I ever learned was the Four Directions Song. There is probably no song that is sung more in the Lakota world than that one. Usually, when it is sung during a gathering, everyone will turn in unison and face the direction being sung to, turning with the song to honor each of the four sacred directions. The sacredness of the number four in Native culture cannot be overstated. The four is in everything. It is the seasons; spring, summer, fall and winter. It is the sacred elements; earth, fire, water and wind. It is the cycle of life; infancy, adolescence, adulthood and elders.

It is the four aspects of the human being; body, soul, mind and spirit. The cardinal directions themselves are fourfold; east, south, west and north. And in more specific ways unique to various Native cultures, there are four sacred colors, plants and animals. As mentioned in the previous chapter, the inipi (sweat lodge) ceremony also follows the four directions. The sacred hoop with four quadrants, also known as the medicine wheel, is a symbol seen in Indigenous cultures around the world. The lessons contained in that hoop are ancient, and impart important knowledge and wisdom about the circle of life, the lunar cycles and the meaning of balance.

When I walked into that Celtic Fire Festival wheel at Brigit's Garden in Ireland and saw the four quadrants – Imbolc, Beltaine, Lughnasa and Samhain – I knew I was witnessing an ancient connection, a synchronistic mystery between two distinct peoples. Imbolc celebrates the coming of spring. Beltaine is the beginning of summer. Lughnasa marks the beginning of the harvest in the autumn. And Samhain is the first of winter, and marks the beginning of the Celtic year. Thus you can see that the Celts too, have an old knowledge of the sacred four.

Being the sum of three and four, seven is a number considered sacred by cultures the world over. This, of course, includes Indigenous peoples and the Celts. In Native culture, the seven directions are the sum of all that is. They are the east, south, west, north, mother earth, father sky and the center. My Lakota brother and friend David Burnette once imparted this wisdom about the seven directions; you cannot fully comprehend the mystery of the seventh direction until you understand the first six. And yet, you cannot understand all the meanings of the first six directions without a knowing of the seventh. Thus, you can see, the seven directions are a circle, a cycle of expansion and ancient wisdom. Seven is the number of the sacred fires of the Lakota. They are the Hunkpapa, Oglala, Sicangu, Sihasapa, MniConjou, Itazipco and Oohenunpa. If the four is what connects us to the earth, then the seven takes us into the deeper places, where the mysteries of sacred power beckon.

Cú Chulainn is the legendary warrior hero god of Celtic mythology. It is said that he had seven fingers on each hand, seven toes on each foot and seven pupils in each of his eyes. He was revered by the Celts for his fearlessness and power in battle. There is a beautiful bronze statue of Cú Chulainn in the General Post Office in Dublin that commemorates the patriots who fought and died for Irish independence in 1916. At all the ancient spiritual places I have been to in Ireland, there are sums of seven, either in the number of stones in a sacred place or in the Neolithic symbols carved into those stones. Beyond the isle of Éire, there are seven seas, seven continents and seven days of the week. In Christian scripture it is said that God rested on the seventh day after creating on the first six. In cultures

21

and nations throughout the world, the seven is considered the ultimate sacred number. It is not lost on me that when the most sacred number of the Celts – the three – and the most sacred number of Indigenous peoples – the four – are joined together, the result is the seven.

Another number considered sacred by the Celts is the number nine. Nine is the culmination of three threes, which alone makes it very special. But most interesting is the fact that, no matter how many times it is multiplied, the nine always comes back to itself. When nine is multiplied by any number, the resulting number always adds up to nine, or eighteen, which is divisible of nine. For example: 2x9=18 and 1+8=9, 9x19=171 and 1+7+1=9, 9x780=7,020 and 7+0+2+0=9 and so on. Try it on a calculator. You'll see it's true. Numbers have power. And the ancients knew the secrets of that power.

As I shared at the start of this chapter, thirteen is the number of lunar cycles in a year. I also mentioned that turtles have thirteen spots on their shells. Many Native people refer to the North American continent as Turtle Island. And Indigenous cultures had names for each of the thirteen moons, each pertaining to their own region and experience with the land. Each of those thirteen lunar cycles has twenty eight days. And you may recall my saying that all buffalo have twenty eight ribs. The number twenty eight is, of course, divisible of four and seven, two of the sacred numbers I have spoken of. The earthbound connections to the celestial world are everywhere, if you know where to look. The ancestors of Native people knew their place in the world. And they knew that place because they knew the stars. The Lakota sometimes refer to themselves as Wicapi Oyate, or Star People, and there are stories that come from a time before memory about an ancient arrival from a distant celestial home. Something about those mysterious stories resonates in me like the music of ancient stars in deep space, singing an almost forgotten song. It is a song the ancient ones knew. We need to hear it again. To sense that vibration of sacred energy that we have lost contact with. To touch once again the mysterious power of sacred numbers and their meanings. To return at long last to the oneness of celestial alignment that whispers to our spirit from the distant, ancestral place of mist and stone.

III

MOTHER EARTH

MYSTICAL MATRIARCHY

The old Lakota was wise. He knew that a man's heart, away from nature, becomes hard. He knew that a lack of respect for growing, living things soon led to lack of respect for humans, too. So he kept his children close to nature's softening influence." These are the words of Luther Standing Bear, a man whose lifespan was such that he was the last known Lakota to kill a buffalo in the old way, and yet lived through America's 'Roaring Twenties' and the Great Depression. In his lifetime, Luther saw changes to the world most of us can only imagine. He watched the old ways of the Lakota, who understood the natural world as nurturer, sustainer and provider, be systematically pushed aside and trampled under by a strange, new people who only saw the earth as a resource to serve and enrich themselves. Luther knew what all Native people once knew; that closeness to the mother softened the soil of the heart and made it possible for seeds of wisdom to be planted there. Mother Earth holds secrets and knowledge that only those who are close to her will learn. Just as Indigenous people of old knew of the celestial connections between the turtle and the buffalo, so there are countless mysteries which are revealed when we draw close to our earth mother with a pure desire to know her. Native people see the earth in its entirety as a living, breathing being. The cycle of seasons is her heartbeat. The winds are her breath. The rivers are her veins. The wetlands are her liver. And the land is her skin. All living things are the offspring of Mother Earth and Father Sky, and thus warrant respect. Human beings are merely a strand in the sacred web of life. Whatever we do to any part of that fragile web, we do to ourselves. All things are connected. Our Mother Earth teaches us that, if we can only listen.

Wind Cave, in western South Dakota, is said to be a birthplace of Lakota people. I have heard stories of the people following a wolf out of the cave to the surface in ancient times. No one knows for sure, but something powerful happened at that place which constituted the birth of a people. I have been there. I have felt its sacred energy. Wind Cave breathes. Some days the air is being drawn into the opening, and other days it is blowing out. It is alive with a life force that cannot be explained with words, only experienced by being there and feeling it for yourself. Such is the way of Mother Earth's sacred places. Mato Tipi (Bear Lodge, a.k.a. 'Devil's Tower') is another such place. I have heard Lakota grandmothers say they won't walk the path around Mato Tipi because its power is so overwhelming that they just fall down. I have spent time at this ancient place too, and that amazing sacred standing stone does indeed hold great power. Again, you must experience it firsthand to touch it. Another sacred place I have been to is Bear Butte. Many prayers and ceremonies have taken place on this venerated hill on the northern Great Plains. Like the Medicine Wheel in Wyoming and the vortexes of Sedona, these ancient sacred places are the spirit doors of Mother Earth. They are the places where the veil that conceals the spirit world from the physical world is thinner, and the impossible becomes possible. But it is not only in these kinds of places that Mother Earth shows us the way. It is in our connection to the sacred elements, cycles and rhythms that we learn from her who we really are, and why we are here. A visit from a special animal, the winds wisping through an old pine, and the message of a fallen feather in our path are all ways in which our earth mother reaches to us and whispers to our spirit. We are not alone. She is calling us to return to her again, to rest upon her bosom and feel her soft embrace. When I was a small boy, my mother would sing to me. I can still hear her voice. I miss it. I long for it. We may not realize it, but we are all longing to hear the sweet voice of our earth mother again. We are missing it. We need it more than ever. Mother Earth is waiting for us to step out our front door and come to visit with her, that our hardened hearts may be softened, and that we may touch that sacred feminine energy, and be better for it.

There is likely no spiritual being revered more by Lakota people than the sacred white buffalo calf woman who brought the sacred pipe and the seven sacred rites to the Lakota in a time before memory. After her visit, she rolled over four times as she departed, each time becoming a different colored buffalo. When she rolled the fourth and final time, she rose as a white buffalo calf. And so you see, it was a woman who imparted the most powerful spiritual aspects of Lakota ways, not a man. That matriarchal thread runs through everything in Lakota culture, and it is the same for most Indigenous peoples I have encountered.

A lot of disinformation and misinformation has been put in books and films concerning the roles and treatment of women in Native cultures. What I have learned and witnessed in my own experience is nothing like what is portrayed in those books and films. I have heard the old stories of how much women were respected and I have seen it firsthand in contemporary settings. Legendary Apache leader Victorio was once asked who the greatest Apache warrior of all time was. His response was quick and unequivocal; it was his sister, Lozen. Lozen was a remarkable, mysterious woman who has been nearly forgotten by history. Her acts of bravery and military ingenuity on the battlefield were unrivaled by any man, Goyahkla (Geronimo) included. She was taken as a prisoner of war after the surrender of Goyahkla, and died of tuberculosis in prison in Alabama at age 49. The Haudenosaunee (Iroquois) people have leaders who are called Clan Mothers. They were and are every bit as important and influential as their male counterparts. In Haudenosaunee as well as Lakota culture (and many Indigenous cultures), when a man married a woman, he went to live with her clan/band, and their children would identify as being from their mother's people. This ancient matriarchy reveals the truth of the position of women in many Native societies of old. Women, grandmothers and motherhood were honored and deeply respected. All Indigenous people know the earth as mother. It is understood that all life springs forth from, and ultimately returns to, mother earth. That knowing instills gentleness in a human being. That relationship and connection with nature softens the heart. As such, Indigenous people were and are inherently kind and long suffering. They have endured unfathomable loss, and yet, have clung fast to those ancient ways which are close to nature, and they know that indeed, the earth is the mother of all.

The Irish are a lot like Native people. They are gentle, gracious and generous. They are thoughtful and kind, loving nothing better than a good laugh. And they too, see the earth as mother and refer to her as such. To the Celts of old, the natural world was the physical manifestation of spiritual truth and power. This maternal relationship with the earth goes back to ancient times. One of the most prominent, prolific and revered deities throughout the ancient Celtic world was the Three Mothers. This triple goddess is usually depicted with three women side by side, and embodies the essence of motherhood and womanhood. There are goddesses of rivers, land and sea, and goddesses of love and war. Perhaps the most famous of all the Celtic deities is the goddess Brigit. There are sacred wells in every corner of Ireland that bear her name. I visited one of these wells during a recent visit to Ireland, and was deeply moved by its seclusion, beauty and energy. The spring fire festival Imbolc is also known as the Festival of Brigit, as she represents peace, protection, abundance and rebirth. Brigit is a fire goddess, as well as the goddess of waters that rise from beneath the earth. The ancient Celts honored her with an eternal flame that was kept burning year round. As the pagan goddess Brigit mysteriously morphed into Saint Brigit of the Catholic faith, the Irish nuns of Kildare continued the thousands of years old custom of keeping Brigit's flame. There were periods where overly fundamental priests had her flame extinguished, considering the custom a relic of Celtic paganism. But on Imbolc in 1992 her eternal flame was relit once again by the Irish Catholic nuns of a new spiritual center in Kildare called Solas Bhríde (Light of Brigit). It remains lit to this day. In the previous chapter I ruminated earlier that the concept of the trinity, and Celtic affinity for the triad, was part of the reason so many become Catholics. I believe another part of that equation was the virgin mother. The reverence Catholicism holds for the Virgin Mary surely rang true to the Celtic way of honoring the mother. In mysterious, mystical ways, the voice of the ancients has continued to whisper to us of their sacred knowledge through the centuries. The Irish are resilient, patient and persistent. They have lost so much of the ancient customs, but still hold on tightly to the remnants of their distant ancestors whose connection to the earth and stars imbued them with fantastic, mystical power.

Ancient Celtic familial systems were, for the most part, patriarchal. And yet, women were not second class citizens by any stretch. Celtic women were equal to men in every sense. They owned and inherited land and property, were equal partners in marriage and were legendary as warriors. Roman writings, from periods of great battles with the Celts, speak of Celtic warrior women with awe, wonder and terror. They marveled at how ferocious these women could be on the battlefield, overpowering Roman soldiers with their wildness and strength time and again. One such woman was the Celtic Queen Boudicca. After her husband's death, it is posited by the Roman historian Publius Cornelius Tacitus that the Romans flogged her and raped her two daughters, as they looted and seized their lands. Boudicca responded to those humiliating indignities by mounting a terrifying revolt that cost over 80,000 Romans their lives. In the end, she was defeated and she and her daughters drank poison to avoid being captured by the Romans. But her mark had been made. There is a bronze sculpture in London of Boudicca and her two daughters on a chariot that celebrates her as a heroine and symbol of freedom and justice. In Roman society, women were little more than chattel, and considered the property of a man. Not so with Celtic women. By comparison, in the Celtic world of old, women had a say in everything and, like Boudicca, some even became rulers. They were never treated as property by any man, husband, father or otherwise.

And a Celtic woman couldn't be forced to marry anyone she didn't wish to. Who she married was her choice, and no one else's. In many ways, Celtic women were freer and more empowered than the liberated women who came a thousand years after them.

And so you can see, both Indigenous and Celtic peoples have long honored and revered the feminine. They both see the earth as a maternal being, and love their homeland as a child loves its mother. Both Celtic and Indigenous women held great power, and wielded it with womanly authority and wisdom. In my experience, Native and Irish women are the strongest women I know. Neither suffers foolishness, nor wilts under duress. Their strength runs deep, with the blood of ancestral warriors, rulers, leaders and queens pumping through their strong hearts. The ancients knew the power of the mother. They whisper of that knowledge from a distant place beyond the mist. The world needs that knowledge today more than ever. We must seek out that elusive whisper that we can barely hear anymore, that we might find our way back to the sacred alignment with the cosmos, the balance of interconnection, and the oneness of all unseen power. Our mother is calling out to us, beckoning us to return to her, to know once again her sacred embrace. Let us go to her and rest our weary head on her shoulder, that the hardness of the world may melt away with her softening touch.

✍

IV

KINDRED SPIRITS

KINDNESS PIERCES THE DARKNESS

In the west of Ireland there is a humble cottage on a small lake that stands frozen in time. Its owner walked out the front door in 1915 and never returned. He was Pádraic Pearse, the educator and poet who would light the fuse that would finally free Ireland from English rule. And when he left his quiet retreat that day, he could not have known that it was the last time he would ever see it, nor that he would become a martyr for Irish independence. I have stood in Pádraic's cottage. It is a beautiful place, which now shares the land with a cultural visitor centre. Something about it gave me the uncanny feeling that Pádraic could come through the door at any moment, returning from a visit with the locals in Ros Muc. But of course, he cannot, in the flesh anyway. During my visit, I could not shake the sense that he was there, watching, listening, whispering. A strange, misty apparition even appeared in a photo I took outside the cottage. It is not a stretch to say, that without Pádraic Pearse, there would be no free Irish republic today. In short, all of Ireland would be part of the United Kingdom, as Northern Ireland remains. When Pádraic left his lovely cottage for the last time, he was on his way to the funeral of a legendary Irish Fenian patriot, Jeremiah O'Donovan Rossa. It was at this funeral that Pádraic would give a rousing oratory of the powerfully moving poem he had composed at his cottage about Irish patriotism and freedom from English rule. It was that speech that lit the spark that ignited the fire of the rising in 1916. During my visit to the cultural visitor centre, a member of the staff told me that Pádraic Pearse's speech was, to the Irish, what Dr. Martin Luther King's *"I have a Dream"* speech was to African Americans. The famous last words of Pádraic's historic oration are, *"Ireland unfree shall never be at peace."*

It seems that on nearly every coast I have ever been to in Ireland there is a centuries old stone tower built by the legendary O'Brien dynasty as a lookout for an attack by sea. I have heard numerous accounts of the mighty O'Brien warriors who successfully resisted the onslaught of the British and Normans for over 500 years. That changed in 1543, when Murrough O'Brien and other Celtic nobles surrendered their Irish royalty to King Henry VIII; A surrender which included an agreement for the Irish to abandon Celtic ways and adopt English laws and customs and swear allegiance to the English crown. Thus began over 400 years of systematic destruction of ancient Celtic culture. I have visited numerous castles and sites across Ireland that still bear the destruction of the notorious Oliver Cromwell, who is responsible for the ethnic cleansing of hundreds of thousands of Irish souls. He is hated by the Irish to this day. Over the centuries, the Irish would rise up on numerous occasions against English occupation and fight fiercely to try and take back Ireland for the Irish, only to see these efforts end in miserable defeat. Then in 1916, a ragtag group of poets, writers, artists and farmers, under the leadership of Pádraic Pearse, mounted a brazen attack against the British military in Dublin. For the most part, these were not fighting men and women, and yet they took up arms and challenged the far superior military force of the English, dreaming once again of a free Ireland. A declaration of Irish Independence was drafted, printed and distributed. From the Dublin General Post Office, which they had occupied and fortified, that declaration was read aloud by Pádraic for anyone within earshot to hear. The rising was short-lived, and those who weren't killed by English soldiers were captured and arrested, including Pádraic Pearse. Most of the Irish people were somewhat complacent, or even slightly annoyed, by the trouble caused as a result of the rising. But that all changed when the English courts charged, tried and executed 14 men within just 10 days. Pádraic Pearse was among them. As the executions continued, the public opinion across Ireland began to turn against the English and in favor of the Irish freedom fighters. In the end, less than 3 years after the rising, in January of 1919, the newly formed Republic of Ireland formally adopted the Irish Declaration of Independence. And for the first time in over 400 years, Ireland was free of British rule (except Northern Ireland, which remains in the U.K.). As I stood in Pádraic's cottage and felt his presence all around me, I could almost see him sitting there at his desk, hammering out the words to a speech that he could not have dreamed would ultimately lead to Irish independence and freedom. It is humbling to stand in the places where history was literally written, and to feel the energy of impassioned souls long gone that changed the world. Pádraic and the others who stood and died for Ireland are more than heroes. They are the voice of the ancient Celts, and the seeds of the mysterious builders of Newgrange, who held the knowledge to move giant stones and form a great circle of power. They tapped into that secret power, and freed their people from beneath a great stone of oppression.

It was -20 degrees Fahrenheit in South Dakota the morning I got on that horse. It was the first day of a 135 mile journey of suffering and sacrifice for about 100 Lakota people. Together we would ride into the blinding cold and frozen prairie to pay homage to our ancestors who had made this terrible trek over a century before. There were breathtaking moments along the way. I will never forget the lonely crunch of my horse's hooves into the frozen snow, as my Sicangu Lakota brother David and I took in the wind swept vastness of our Lakota homeland. And I will always remember the camaraderie and togetherness I felt with all those I rode alongside. The destination of our journey was Wounded Knee, a place of great sorrow. In December of 1890, after the Indigenous people of the Americas had suffered 400 years of relentless genocidal assault, deliberate ethnic cleansing and endless forced removals from ancestral lands, a final cruel blow was dealt to a few hundred desperate, unarmed and starving Lakota people. They were massacred by the infamous 7th Cavalry and buried in a mass grave at a place called Wounded Knee. That grave was our destination. We would ride there, as they have every year since 1986, to do what we could to try and heal, collectively and individually. I can tell you it was a healing experience for me. I have stood at Wounded Knee and heard Lakota grandmothers weep as they told of their deep pain and loss. And Lakota people are not alone. Native peoples from sea to shining sea have endured great loss and suffered terrible oppression.

A few years ago a protest sprang up against an oil pipeline that was moving toward the Missouri River, just north of the Standing Rock Lakota Sioux reservation. Thousands of Indigenous people descended on a small parcel of land near the river, and a standoff began that lasted many months. I was there. A lot was happening, but there is something I remember most from my time there. At the camp where I stayed, there was a gathering each night. About two dozen Native people from many different nations would make a circle around the fire and, one by one, each person would share. I came away from my time at the Standing Rock protest camp with something that was made painfully clear during those nightly fire gatherings – Native people are hurting, and a great healing is needed. There were a lot of tears shed around that fire each night, even from seemingly hardened old men.

President Andrew Jackson is responsible for the ethnic cleansing of countless tens of thousands of Native people. The so-called 'Trail of Tears' was the direct result of Jackson's 'Indian Removal Act'. One of the many tribal nations that were forcibly removed from their homelands was the Cherokee. As the vast majority of Cherokee people were rounded up and forced from their homes at gunpoint, a small number of them were slipping away and disappearing into hiding places deep in the Smoky Mountains. I have heard stories from Cherokee friends about the Irish who lived nearby, sneaking supplies to the hidden Cherokee people in the dead of night, and even taking Cherokee babies into their homes during that terrible time. After the fervor of the forced removal subsided, and the hidden Cherokee were reasonably safe to come out of hiding, they reorganized. But they had no land. It was a Welsh-Irish man named William Thomas who purchased the land that eventually became the Qualla Boundary, the land-base of what is today the Eastern Band Cherokee Nation.

As I mentioned previously, my McGuire and O'Farrell ancestors emigrated from Ireland to America during the Great Hunger, also known as the Irish Potato Famine. In truth, the famine was less a natural disaster and more a direct result of the social construct and colonial policies controlled by Britain. Approximately 1 million people died, and another million emigrated because of the famine. My ancestors, Ann O'Farrell and John McGuire, were among that second million. Their family and friends were surely among the first. During a recent visit to Ireland, my wife and I stayed an entire month in a wonderful pre-famine thatched cottage in Galway called 'An Buntsop'. While there we made several trips to a lovely small village called Kinvara. Each time we would approach the town I noticed a small sign that said *'The Great Famine "Mass Grave" 1840s'*. Finally, on our last visit to Kinvara, we stopped and drove the narrow lane down to the cemetery. At first, I didn't see them. But as I made my way to the rear of the graveyard they came into view; dozens of small, round stones, worn by age and the elements, nearly covered over by grass. There were no inscriptions and no flowers. Only a large, rectangular stone at the back edge of the mass grave that was inscribed with these words: *"To the memory of unnamed victims of famine who died during 1845 – 47 at Foys House and were buried here."* It is a sad and desolate place that felt strangely similar to the mass grave at Wounded Knee. I have made a promise to myself that the next time I visit Ireland I will lay flowers at every famine gravestone in that cemetery.

Another tribal nation that endured forced removal during the 'Trail of Tears' was the Choctaw. Some of the Choctaw people were potato farmers. In 1847, little more than a decade after they had been forced to leave their homeland in what is now

Mississippi, the Choctaw began to hear stories of the terrible potato famine in Ireland. They were told that things were so desperate that the Irish were eating leaves and grass to try and stay alive. The Choctaw remembered the starvation and death they suffered during the removal march, and they felt empathy and compassion for these people from across the seas who also were potato growers. The Choctaw had very little money, but they decided to do what they could to help the Irish. They gathered $170 (between $5,000 and $6,000 in today's money) and sent it to Ireland. That act of compassion was never forgotten by the Irish. Today, there is a bi-national organization called CAIT, *Celts & American Indians Together* that honors the historic connection of compassion between the Choctaw and Ireland by raising millions of dollars for world famine relief. There is a wonderful book by Marie-Louise Fitzpatrick about this story called *'The Long March'*. It is brilliantly illustrated by award winning Choctaw artist Gary WhiteDeer. In 2020, with the global pandemic hitting the Navajo people especially hard, the Irish raised over 2 million dollars to help the Navajo and Hopi nations. One Irish donor put it this way, "You helped us in our darkest hour. Honored to return the kindness. Ireland remembers, with thanks."

Both the Celts and Indigenous people have suffered oppression. Both have been considered trouble by the powers that be. There was the 'Indian Problem' and the 'Irish Problem' in America. Each has had to fight and die for their ancestral homeland. Irish and Native people have had to battle against distorted stereotypes that portray them in ways that are at best one dimensional, and at worst utterly offensive and ridiculous. Both are earth based, circular peoples who were considered uncivilized savages by their oppressors. I have stood and wept at mass gravesites of Native people in America and Irish people in Ireland. The two are an ocean apart, but their suffering is the same. They have a shared oppression that binds them together in a mysterious way. They understand each other. They know each other's pain, thus can see each other's humanity. The loss each has endured has birthed compassion in the other. For there is no greater act of empathy than that moment when kindness pierces the darkness and heals the soul.

Oh, and by the way, in 2017 a beautiful sculpture featuring nine feathers by Irish artist Alex Pentek was unveiled in Cork, Ireland in honor of the historic relationship of kindness between the Choctaw and the Irish. The sculpture is entitled *Kindred Spirits*.

Victors and Heroes

Ten blue jays and a cardinal landed in a distant tree outside my window.
I am thinking about Irish rain.
It is cloudy today and my thoughts are disjointed.
A memory of a small country church on the Pine Ridge Indian Reservation and a cottage built across the sea for an innocent activist as a refuge from his strong conviction.
In the comfort of my room surrounded by nothing, I listen and count my feathered friends.
That church and cottage, though oceans and miles apart, come together in my mind and form the waves upon which my stagnated dreams flow.
My arms are stretched to reach the choir and the solo, the surrendered and the martyr.
They reach to touch heroism and courage, of which my small life requires none.
But I am an admirer of bravery and sacrifice, even if not a participant.
I stand in awe of the ones who swallowed their pride to feed their children and the ones who gave their lives to free a nation.
Both victors, both heroes.
As I watch the blue jays and wonder why so many have gathered as a prologue to my thoughts.

Peggy Perry-Hill

V

HONOR & VALOR

COURAGE AND GENEROSITY

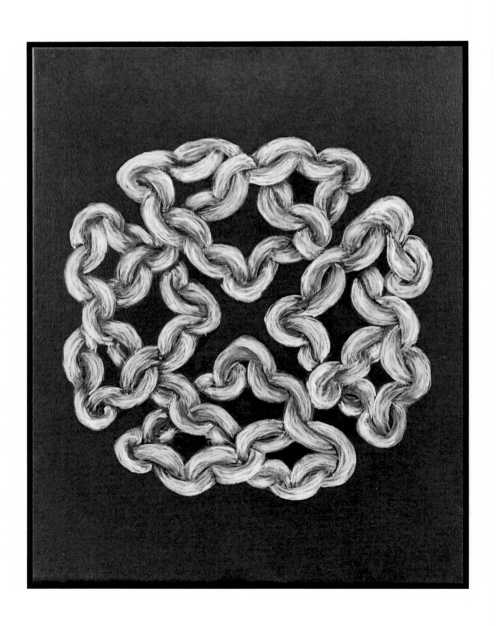

Always do the right thing, no matter the cost. In the Celtic world there was arguably no more important ethic than honor. It was so important that all other Gaelic values, like hospitality, loyalty, honesty, generosity, justice and courage were based around it. In ancient times, Féineachas, or Brehon Law was the code of ethics and conduct that Celtic people lived by. It was a system anchored in honor. It is said that, in the olden days, to be inhospitable to a stranger was such a dishonorable act that it could incur a 'geis', or curse which would cause the perpetrator to never deny anyone hospitality ever again. This cultural code continues into the present, as the Irish are well known as a welcoming people. I have experienced this firsthand. Wherever I have been in Ireland, complete strangers have opened their hearts and homes, and given of their time, nearly always offering a cup of tea. The good people at An Buntsop Cottage in Galway treated us like we were family. And every time we have ever been to Ireland, our dear friends of the Servants of Love monastic community in Wicklow have always welcomed us to stay and spend time at their place, feeding us and treating us as one of their own. There is a lovely craft village north of Galway in a town called An Spidéal (or Spiddal). We happened on it on one of our drives during our most recent stay in Ireland, and loved it so much we just kept coming back. It was at this craft village that we made a couple new friends at the Glass Craft shop, Dee and Sue. We popped in on them several times over the course of a couple weeks. On our final visit to their store, Sue surprised me with a gift. She had created a beautiful stained glass medicine wheel with a Celtic swirl in the center. I was deeply touched. I still am. That Irish-made Native-Celtic four directions wheel still hangs in a special place of honor in my home. The Irish have been through so much. But through it all they never lost their kindness.

In my view, the oppression of both Celtic and Indigenous people was made possible in part because of their shared natural tendency to welcome and give the benefit of the doubt to a stranger. Ironically, this innate and honorable quality of selflessness made them both vulnerable to those with selfish motives. There is an old saying in Ireland about those who come to live among them becoming "More Irish than the Irish themselves." This sentiment is a testament to the age old Celtic way of hospitality and generosity. The Normans are a great example of this. They invaded and settled in Ireland in the 12th century. And though at first they maintained their own distinct culture, after a century or two, they had so taken on the Gaelic customs and ways that it was said they had become more Irish than the Irish themselves. The Normans became so infused into Gaelic life that many of their surnames live on in Irish families today; names like Fitzgerald, FitzGibbons, Devereux, D'Arcy, Lacy, Morrell, Barry and Burke. All of this speaks to that intangible Irish quality of endearment, acceptance and their welcoming spirit.

The same can be said of Indigenous people; regardless of how slim things might be financially, if you come to visit they will find a way to feed you. During a recent trip to Pine Ridge Indian reservation in South Dakota, we paid a visit to our niece, Suzette Thunder Hawk and her family. We did not come expecting to be fed, only to see everyone and spend time with them. But upon our arrival, it was plain to see that our dear Suzette had been at it all day, preparing a turkey dinner with all the fixings. We had a wonderful visit and a delicious meal. This is the way of Native people. It is an old way of generosity, hospitality and honor. Before we left that day, they gifted me a beautiful handmade necklace, and an amazing hand beaded bracelet. I wear both of these gifts often, and when I do, I feel their love, kindness and generosity.

In old times, the Lakota and Crow were enemies. One of the ways they would cause trouble for one another was to steal each other's horses. It was a practice that had gone on for generations. And it was risky, because if you were caught, you could be wounded or even killed. One moonlit night, two Lakota scouts were watching their sleeping encampment from a nearby hill, when one of them spotted movement below. As they watched intently, it became clear that a Crow man was stealthily working his way around the edge of the camp, rounding up horses as he went. The two Lakota scouts prepared to head him off at the pass once he was on his way. But something unexpected happened just as the Crow man was about to escape with their horses. A frail Lakota unci (grandmother) came out of her tipi and began to struggle in her effort to gather some wood from a woodpile. As the two Lakota men looked on from the hill, they saw a moral dilemma unfolding. The Crow man had stopped, and was watching the grandmother from his hidden vantage point. It became clear that he was struggling with what decision he should make. Help the old woman, or make off with the horses? Surely he must have known that he would receive great praise from his people for having succeeded at taking so many horses from the Lakota. He also knew that, by revealing himself to help this elder, he risked not only losing the horses, but his life. And yet, as the two Lakota men watched in amazement from the hillside, the Crow man quietly made his way out of the darkness toward the old woman, and then helped her with the wood. The Lakota grandmother surely knew that he was Crow, and that there was only one reason a Crow man would be anywhere near a Lakota camp in the middle of the night. But she alerted no one of his presence, and accepted his help. Once she was back inside her tipi, he crept back out of sight and proceeded to make his way out of the area with the horses. Now the Lakota scouts had a dilemma. Having just watched this man risk everything to help an elder, they decided that this was a man of great honor. This was a man who deserved to be met face to face on the battlefield some day, not ambushed in the dead of night. And so they let him, and their horses, go. This is a story of honor. From battles, to relationships, to leadership, honor has always been at the center of everything in the world of Indigenous people.

✍

Oliver Cromwell's strategic method to winning at warfare was to literally kill everyone. That was not the way of the Celts. The Celtic warrior was bound by honor and valor. Victory was achieved by showing oneself stronger and more courageous than your enemy in battle. A Celtic warrior did not harm the innocent, but preferred to do battle face to face with a worthy adversary. It should be noted here that Celtic warriors were both male and female, and both were legendary on the battlefield.

Indigenous peoples like the Lakota and Crow had fought with each other for centuries. And like the ancient Celt, the custom of the Native warrior was a way of honor and valor. For example, the greatest act of courage a Lakota warrior could perform in battle was not to kill, but to be the first to count a non lethal 'strike' with a wooden stick on an enemy combatant. That strike sent a message to your enemies that you were not afraid of them, and that you had the courage to meet them face to face. Like Cromwell, the armies of soldiers that Indigenous warriors would face off with time and again over the course of a century believed that killing was winning. And again, like the Celts, that was just not the way of Indigenous warriors. They just could not conceive of battle without a code of honor.

What both Indigenous and Celtic warriors had in common was that they belonged to peoples who knew the value of a life, whether human, animal or plant. You see, at its core, hospitality is the welcoming of the 'other'. It is the ability to open your heart to see the humanity in a stranger. And it is that quality in both the ancient Celts and Indigenous peoples which predisposed them to seeing the humanity even in their enemies.

As I covered previously, when a Lakota man married a Lakota woman, he went to live with her people. The tipi was her domain, and their children belonged to her band. Not to mention that a man was required to prove his worthiness and earn the approval of the woman's father and family by way of gifts of horses or meat before he could be married to her. If a Lakota woman decided that her husband was no good, he would return from a hunt or some other excursion to find all his belongings sitting outside the door of the tipi. This was a great dishonor and brought shame upon him as a Lakota man. But there was a way for him to restore his honor. He could gift the new husband of his former wife with horses. Can you imagine such a practice today? This old traditional custom demonstrates how very important honor was to Indigenous people.

In ancient Irish law there was a custom called *troscud* (fasting). When a member of the lower class had been wronged by someone of the higher class, they could conduct a *troscud* outside the home of the wrong-doer, fasting from food or drink from morning till night where all in the community could see. The honorable thing for the more privileged wrong-doer to do was to come out and hear the grievance of the person doing the fasting and try to resolve the matter. If they did not, and chose to stay in their home and enjoy the day's meals while there was a person they had wronged fasting outside, it was considered a very dishonorable act that would result in moral condemnation. This custom is just one among many in the Celtic world that maintained a balance of power, encouraged fairness and rewarded honor.

Irish and Native people continue to place great value on honor and valor today. They are generous, loyal, hospitable and kind, and try to see the good in others; even those they don't agree with or understand. For at their center, both cultures have an ancient knowledge of the interconnection of all things, and thus recognize that the life force which hums in all living beings is a powerful, sacred circular energy that warrants great respect.

VI

TALKING TREES

MESSENGERS

Imagine a strange tree in an ancient Irish forest. Some branches are cut, some are not. There are a few on one side, and a few on the other; some straight out, some pointing down. What could it mean? What could it be? It is a sign, a message in the sacred Celtic Tree alphabet known as Ogham, which was once known only to the mysterious and powerful Druids. The Ogham writing is a language of talking trees. The writing itself has the appearance of a tree, with a center line like a trunk, and horizontal lines like branches to form letters and words. I first saw the Ogham as a Stone Age carving, and then in shops throughout Ireland. I have heard it said that the Druids would leave messages for each other in the forest by cutting a tree into an Ogham word that no one else could comprehend. Like the Druids themselves, the Ogham draws its power from the trees and the natural world. And this ancient language still holds a mystical energy that can whisper secrets into the soul, as I discovered one blessed day in Ireland.

One of my Irish family names, McGuire is a modern spelling of the Gaelic *Mag Uidhir*, which means "son of the dark one". Another modern spelling is Maguire. Just across the border into Northern Ireland is a place called Enniskillen in County Fermanagh. From the late 1200s to the early 1500s, Fermanagh was the domain of Maguire kings. There is a castle there that was built in the early 1400s by a Maguire. I have stood in that castle and touched its ancient stone walls, hoping to reach through time and connect in some unexplainable way to my Celtic ancestors. I am always trying to connect to what was. I can't explain it, but something in me has always longed to hear that voice that whispers on the other side of the mist of forgotten ages. I am deeply proud to be of the ancient Celtic *Mag Uidhir* lineage. And I felt a strong connection to my ancestors that day in Enniskillen. But it would be the mysterious Ogham that would reach through the ether and impart to me a priceless gift of deep and ancient connection to my Celtic forebears in a most unexpected way.

The Aran Islands are a group of three islands (Inishmore, Inishmaan and Inisheer) just off the west coast of Ireland, and going there is like traveling back in time. Most of the residents speak Gaelic, and the pace is slower, more in keeping with the gentle motion of the ocean waves washing in and out from the shore. To get there, I took a ferry with my wife, Peggy, and my dear Irish friend, Brother Seamus. I have always had issues with motion sickness, so the ferry ride across the choppy sea left little to be desired. But I held it together and gladly stepped onto the island of Inisheer into another world. We took a lovely horse drawn tour around the island with a lively Gaelic speaking fellow named Joe, visited an O'Brien castle ruin, popped into a few small shops and had a bite to eat. When it was nearing time to catch our return ferry, Seamus and Peggy took a walk down to the water's edge to dip their feet in while we waited. As they walked off I began to hear a tapping sound that drew my attention to a red haired man in a kilt nearby who was working away at some craft. As I approached, it became clear to me what he was doing. He was carving Ogham words into small stone tablets with a chisel and hammer. The little tablets all had a hole in the top so they could be strung onto a leather necklace. He looked up at me from his work and said hello, and then asked me if I would like him to make me something. I didn't hesitate. I asked him if he could carve my ancestral Celtic family name, Mag Uidhir, in Ogham, onto one of those small stone tablets. He told me that would be no problem. As the ferry was set to leave in less than half an hour, I then asked him, "Can you do it in 20 minutes?" He responded, "I sure can!", and got busy! He finished in the nick of time and strung it on a leather strap for me. I paid him and thanked him as I turned to hustle back to the ferry and pulled my new Mag Uidhir Ogham necklace over my head and onto my neck. On the return ferry ride, Seamus and I went up top behind the captain's cabin. I showed him my new necklace, and when he saw it he said something I will never forget. He said, "You cannot get more ancient Celtic than that." A curious thing happened on the return ferry ride; I had no motion sickness. I shared that with Seamus as we held on with the strong wind and the rocking of the boat. He told me with a smile as we laughed, "It's your McGuire ancestors coming through!" Those words, though spoken in jest, rang true somehow. Something about that little stone tablet resting against my chest affirmed something deep in my soul that day, and has never left me since: I am a Celt. I am Irish. I am a McGuire, an O'Farrell and a Kelly. I carry the blood, the stories, and the spirit of my Celtic-Irish ancestors, and an indelible connection to the land from which they came. And somehow, someway, it was the mysterious, ancient Ogham, the ancient Celtic Tree language, that turned my ear to a tapping sound on the shore that day, and whispered the truth of connection that brought my spirit full circle.

Since 1999, I have made my home in the Ozark Mountains of Arkansas just outside of a wonderful little historic town of artists, musicians, hippies and free thinkers called Eureka Springs. The small city comes by its name because it was built on and around a myriad of springs. The Indigenous people of the Osage, Quapaw, Caddo and other nations from the region considered the area that is now Eureka Springs sacred, thus they would never live there, only visiting when there was a need. The springs once held mysterious healing powers, which the Native people knew and understood. *Sweet Spring* got its name because it was said the water tasted like it had sugar in it. The *Basin Spring* was shaped like a basin and had healing properties. And there is a written record of a young woman who had her sight restored after an Osage medicine man directed her to wash her eyes in the waters of a sacred spring that is now called *Harding Spring*. There is *Crescent Spring, The Grotto* and numerous others all throughout the city. On the outskirts of town there is another special spring called *Magnetic*. There is a street named after it. On the corner of Magnetic and Main Street is a lovely little shop called *Ice Cream Delights*, which is owned and operated by our friends Richard and Shirley. Peggy and I love to go there and get Shirley's famous Vegetable Soup, Grilled Cheese and Rueben Sandwich while we visit with them. And of course we almost always finish up with an ice cream soda! If you stand in the right place outside of Richard and Shirley's shop, you can spot two very interesting trees, the first on the other side of Main, and the second just up Magnetic. They are older trees, and both have trunks that bend 90 degrees and become horizontal about halfway up and then bend another 90 degrees and continue vertically upward. These are talking trees. They are shaped that way today because a very long time ago, a Native person bent it over and tied it to the ground as a sort of sign, pointing the way to something. In this case, the first tree points to the second tree. And the second points to *Magnetic Spring*, which gets its name because in the old days, you could hold a metal pipe under the water for a few minutes, and then the pipe could pick up nails it had become so magnetized. Talking trees, like these two pointer trees in Eureka Springs, can be found in countless locations across North America.

In the Lakota language they are called chan. They are called crann in the Gaelic. They are the trees, the sacred standing people, and they have always been treated with reverence by both Indigenous and Celtic cultures. My involvement in and around Lakota tradition has taught me to be respectful of the life force of all the plant peoples, and that includes the trees. Out on the vast Great Plains there are not a lot of wooded areas, but there is a special tree that grows everywhere in that region, and is considered very sacred by Lakota people. That tree is the cottonwood, and it is placed in the center of the circle at all Lakota sun dance ceremonies. I won't get into specifics here, but there is a very detailed, sacred manner in which the cottonwood is chosen, felled, carried and prepared for this. Cedar and red willow trees also have spiritual meaning to the Lakota and other Native peoples. The sprigs of the cedar are a medicine, and are one of the four sacred plants used in many prayer rites. The red willow is the preferred tree with which to build the sweat lodge, and its smaller branches were once exclusively used to make a small sacred item known as the dreamcatcher. Indigenous people have long understood that the standing people are our relatives, and that without them we perish. The old ones also knew that the trees of the primeval forests that once stood deep and dense on this earth were interconnected in mysterious ways to us, and to one another, giving life to all. The best example of this I have ever seen was the depiction of 'The Tree of Souls' in the movie Avatar. There is a powerful, life sustaining energy in trees that warrants our respect. Indigenous people have known that since a time before memory. There is a spiritual custom that many Native cultures practice in which a pinch of tobacco or other sacred herb is placed into a red cloth, fashioned into a ball and tied with sinew. This little item is called a prayer tie, and they are often fastened to the branch of a tree near a sacred site. Visit any of the ancient, sacred places in the Americas I have mentioned, and you will see these red prayer ties hanging from trees everywhere.

Like Indigenous people, the ancient Celts had respect for the trees, and held some of them in high esteem as especially sacred. The druids considered the oak to be very powerful, and they were known to conduct mysterious ceremonies around them. The mistletoe was also revered by the druids. Another tree which the Celts of old and the Irish to this day hold a wary respect for is the Hawthorn, also known as The Fairy Tree. It is said that to cut one down is to risk terrible misfortune. And I have heard that new roads in Ireland have even been rerouted to avoid having to remove one of these mysteriously enchanted trees. In yet another fascinating synchronicity between the Celts and Indigenous people, I have heard that, at certain sacred wells where there is either a Hawthorn or an Ash tree, strips of red cloth are tied to the branches and left as prayer offerings. And during our first visit of many to Brigit's Garden, we happened upon a tree filled with hundreds of small prayer cards tied on with a ribbon. Again, the hidden connections abound.

There is a tree in the forest by my home that I call 'The Teacher'. I have taken people to visit this tree who are emotionally broken or hurting in some way. The tree is a pine, and it is twisted and contorted, yet still has grown to a great height. The reason for its peculiar shape is that it happened to grow up under what was once a barbed wire fence. The fence is long gone, but the barbed wire is still there, going in one side of the tree and coming out the other. That tree had to struggle mightily to survive, but it did, against all odds. And there it stands as a quiet example of what is possible if we keep reaching for the light. I am like that tree, as are many others who have been to see it, and went away wiping tears of healing from their eyes.

You've likely seen them both. Today they are usually in the form of jewelry, art or a decoration. Their original meanings and purposes are lost on most folks these days. But both the ancient Celtic Shield Knot and Native American Dreamcatcher have sacred origins, and still hold the spiritual powers they once knew before our modern society dismissed and trivialized them. There are many variations of the Celtic Shield

Knot, but all of them mimic the winding roots of the Oak tree; the most sacred of all trees to the Druids. The Shield Knot has no beginning or end, which imbues it with the humming essence of infinity. And it has four points, an obvious tie to the four cardinal directions and the four Fire Festivals of the Celtic world, Imbolc, Beltaine, Lughnasad and Samhain. The Shield Knot is so named because it was once carried on the shields of Celtic warriors for protection against their foes in battle. For the spiritual power of the sacred Shield Knot is just that: protection. Various forms of the knot were carried by children to protect them from bad or evil spirits, and it was also used by the sick to ward off dark energy and make space for healing. The Shield Knot is one of the oldest and most sacred of all Celtic knots, and versions of it can be seen in everything from ancient stone carvings, to Celtic crosses to the legendary Book of Kells. Modern depictions of the Shield Knot are everywhere. And most people see them as little more than a cool art style that pays homage to Irish culture. But right there, under the surface of all Celtic Shield Knots, still lies the ancient, sacred power of spiritual protection. The Native American Dreamcatcher came to be in a time before memory. Many Indigenous nations have a version of the Dreamcatcher, and an origin story to go with it. Suffice it to say that the Dreamcatcher was manifested through a vision in a time of peril and infused with the spiritual power of protection from bad spirits and dark dreams. A small, circular hoop with a webbed center, it was made from a thin branch and the sinew of the deer. A feather was often attached to the bottom. They were hung over the places where children slept, to protect them from bad visions and dreams, allowing only the good to pass through the hole in the center of the web. The result is an entire generation that grows up with good dreams and visions for the future of their people. Today, the sacred Dreamcatcher has been sadly reduced to a cute, novelty item to hang from a rear view mirror, or on a wall as a decoration. Very few know of its origin or its sacred power. But like the Celtic Shield Knot, the Native American Dreamcatcher still holds its ancient spiritual energy of protection. Thus you can see that both the ancient Celts and Indigenous people utilized the trees to communicate, send messages and offer protection. This interwoven relationship with the natural world runs like a thread through both cultures, weaving the protective Native dreamcatcher and the Celtic Shield Knot together in a mysterious way that binds the two as one. And if we learn to honor these sacred talismans, and seek to understand their origins, we can once again gain access to their ancient power.

I grew up in the woods. I spent a lot of time out there with my dad, who liked to hunt the old way, close to the ground with respect. One morning when we were about to head into the woods, my dad taught me something I have always remembered. He said that we needed to move slow and become one with the forest as we entered it, and that if we moved too quickly or made too much noise, the ravens who were sitting high atop the trees would notice us, and fly off to warn all the animals in the woods that we were there. I marveled at that lesson of interconnection. And it taught me to slow down, to breathe in the moments, and connect with the natural world and find myself in it. I have heard it said that the old Lakota grandmothers could talk with the ravens. I believe it. It was a raven that perched itself on the top of the tunnel leading into the factory where I worked all those years ago, and cawed its warning to me nearly every day, until I finally made the decision to quit that job and take a chance on my music. I still think about that raven sometimes when I am about to take the stage at a concert.

Plains Indian people have an old relationship with the Eagle. In Lakota the eagle is called wanbli, and revered as a most sacred bird. Its feathers were collected and given as high honors to those who had shown their courage or selflessness. I have heard it said that one eagle feather held the value of forty horses. The eagle bonnet worn by highly esteemed leaders was a powerful statement about their heroic deeds and their sacrifices for the people. It took a man a lifetime to earn those eagle feathers. This is why it is so foolish and disrespectful for anyone to don a mock eagle bonnet to play dress up for vanity or recreation. These things are personal, sacred and hold an ancient power that should not be trifled with. Another messenger is the owl. It is said by certain Native cultures that if an owl visits you in the daytime and looks at you, it is an omen that someone close to you is about to make their journey to the spirit world. This message is not considered 'evil', as death is understood by Indigenous people as a part of the sacred circle of life. Rather, this particular kind of visit from the owl is seen as a blessing, as it gives us a chance to prepare. I experienced this phenomenon myself. An owl visited me in the daylight and looked right at me shortly before my father died at age 54. And it happened again the following year when my mother died at age 51. A visit from a rabbit is a reminder to stay humble. The wolf is the teacher, one who shows the way out of the darkness, like the wolf in Wind Cave, leading the people into the light of a new day. The bear is the nurturer, provider and fierce protector. And a visit from one might portend a need for you to address one of these areas in your life. These kinds of messengers are unexplainable, but they are very real.

In the Celtic world of old, there were animal and bird messengers as well. It was said that if a lone magpie showed up cackling at your door and looked directly at you, it was bringing a message of death. However, if two magpies came to visit, they brought a blessing of prosperity. The robin redbreast was considered very sacred by the Celts. To kill one would ensure that you would never have good luck again, even if you lived a thousand years. There were a myriad of foretelling messages that involved cats – usually as bad omens – as cats are very prolific in Ireland. The wren is known as the bird of the Druids, as to know its language is to possess the knowledge of coming events which the wren imparts. And yet, ironically, the wren has long been hated by the Irish. As the story goes, an Irish army was quietly moving into position for an attack on the notorious Oliver Cromwell, when suddenly a flock of wrens landed on their drums and began pecking away on the drumheads. The disturbance alerted Cromwell's men of their approach, after which not one of the Irish men survived. The cricket has long been considered by the Celts to be enchanted, possessing an ancient knowledge and wisdom. It is said that if we could understand the language of the cricket, we would stand to learn a great deal. To have one in your home was considered lucky, and they were never killed. The Celts recognized that a sacred communication with birds and animals was part and parcel of an ancient connection with nature, and they took notice of that connection wherever they saw it.

For my wife, Peggy, the buck deer is a sacred messenger. She has had many strange and mysterious visits with them over the years, some of which I have witnessed. We have two sweat lodges on our land, one for women and one for men. They are both in the woods near our private driveway. One afternoon we were returning home from a trip to town when we saw something remarkable. As we pulled down our driveway and the women's lodge came into view, we were stunned to see a buck deer with a very large rack of antlers sitting inside the frame of the lodge. We slowed to a stop and looked on in amazement. The buck turned to look back at us, but never moved. How he managed to maneuver his way inside that wooden framed dome with that huge head of horns is still a mystery to me. And the fact that he hardly reacted at all to our presence was equally fascinating. There was something meaningful imparted to Peggy during that visit with the buck inside the lodge frame that day. These kinds of moments of interaction allow us to plug in to something deep and ancient that binds our spirit with the circular, swirling energy of the cosmos.

There are messengers in our world. We live our lives with an awareness and understanding of three dimensions. But there are other dimensions beyond our scope, beyond our comprehension, that sometimes intersect with our three dimensional experience and touch us in unexplainable ways. That moment when a special bird pays you a visit, just when you need it, is real. And sometimes a visit from a bird or an animal is more than a coincidence. Sometimes it is a message. I mentioned previously that I am a pragmatic person, and that I don't automatically believe everything I hear.

If you are like me, then let me tell you this: I do not know how it works, and I honestly don't really care. I just know from personal experience that messengers from the natural world are real. Somehow, someway they whisper to us from another dimension beyond the veil.

❧

One of the coolest things about the McGuire family crest is that it features a warrior on a white horse. As a person of Lakota lineage who has taken part in a 135 mile pilgrimage on the back of a horse; and as the Lakota people are historically a horse culture, I find that connection to be very special. As it turns out, the relationship with the horse is yet another thing the Celts and Indigenous people have in common. Both Celtic and Native warriors were legendary horsemen. The ancient Celts have been described as a nation of horsemen, as have the Lakota and other Native American peoples. And both cultures treated their horses with gentleness and great respect, never mistreating them. Imagery of the horse is highly prevalent in many Native cultures. Horses appear in the ancient winter counts and in ledger art. They were painted on the outside of Plains Indian tipis, and displayed on shields and regalia. When the beloved horse of a Lakota warrior died, he would honor his fallen comrade by creating a horse stick in his horse's likeness. Specific designs and adornments were added to the horse stick to help tell the story of his horse's heroism and courage. All of this was done with the hope that the spirit of his horse would bestow its strength upon the warrior and remain with him throughout his life. The Celts honored their horses as well. From trumpets with the ends fashioned into the shape of a horse's head to carvings of four horsemen into the sheaths of ancient Celtic swords, depictions of horses were prolific in Celtic culture. Undeniably the most impressive depiction of a horse the Celts ever created is the 360 foot (110 meters) long, prehistoric White Horse hill figure in Uffington, England. Over 3,000 years old, the enormous horse image was formed by cutting trenches at least 3 feet deep into the hillside and filling them with crushed white chalk. This ancient Celtic White Horse figure is so impressive it can be seen from 20 miles away. During our stay at An Buntsop Cottage in Galway, there was a gorgeous white horse in a nearby pasture that we passed nearly every day. It wasn't lost on me that the McGuire horse was white. As I said before, the synchronicities abound.

I saw the old man sitting alone at the powwow, so I approached him and said hello. It turned out he was Cherokee, and we started into a long, friendly chat. At one point we stumbled onto a conversation about a certain Native American museum and historic site. I mentioned that there was a large portion of the history the museum claimed was unknown. The old man's reply took me by surprise. He said curtly, "That's because they won't listen to our oral history." He went on that day to explain in significant detail the oral history he knew that perfectly filled in the period the museum claimed was 'unknown'. It was a fascinating visit that I have never forgotten. The storytellers in Indigenous cultures were the historians, the genealogists and the entertainers. They were revered and honored, as they carried the entire history of the nation in their memories. Their most important job was to ensure that all that information was passed on to the next generation fully intact. And for countless centuries they did just that, without fail. I have sat at the fireside with my ciye (older brother) Chubbs Thunder Hawk and had him impart to me the oral history that was passed on to him by an old storyteller when he was young. That ancient custom of keeping the stories lives on. And those oral history lessons continue to be told in the inner circles of Native family and community life. Those songs, the stories and the history are the whispers of an ancient way of life that once held great power, and beckons us back into the mists of a forgotten time. That old way is the lifeblood of the culture, traditions and customs of the people. It is the thread that ties the present and future to the past. Without it, I believe all would be lost.

It was the poets who were the story keepers in the Celtic world. Like Indigenous storytellers, the poets held the entire history and genealogy of the Celtic people in their memories. I have heard it said that the poets could recite a poem with over 1,000 lines from memory. On top of that, they also knew countless songs, and could compose their prose and singing in such a way as to entertain, educate and illuminate all at the same time during important gatherings. The poets also held great political power, as their words were revered, and could either heap praise or bring condemnation down on any Celtic noble. In the Celtic way, possessing oratory eloquence was considered far more powerful than physical strength and prowess. As such, the poets wielded authority and might with the mere utterance of a word. These gifted wordsmiths of story and song are the voice of an ancient people, calling out from beyond the stones, harkening us back to the sacred knowledge and wisdom of spirit messengers and mysterious talking trees. A great truth awaits us there: An ancient connection with our primal heart, and a return to oneness with all that is.

VII

DRUIDS & MEDICINE PEOPLE

MYSTERY, KNOWLEDGE
AND POWER

In flowing white robes they gathered around an old oak tree to conduct the ceremonial gathering of the sacred mistletoe. As one climbed the oak and cut the revered plant with a gold knife, the others formed a circle and held a white cloth below to catch it and prevent it from touching the ground. Two white bulls were then sacrificed, as prayers were offered that the freshly cut mistletoe might achieve its full medicinal power. This is from an actual eye witness account of a druidic ceremony that occurred some 2,000 years ago in about 50 A.D. It is the earliest known account of such a rite, but it is accepted that the druids were well established in ancient Celtic areas long before that. How long ago the powerful, sacred order of the druids existed is unknown. Even the word 'druid', though ancient, is not near as old as the order itself. The word druid appears to be a derivative of two words. The first syllable, 'dru' refers to the oak tree, which has always held mystical powers for the Celts. The second syllable, 'wid', means 'to know'. Thus the two joined together as 'dru-wid' or druid surely means "knowledge of the oak." The druids are known to have possessed a vast understanding of the cosmos and the physics of the natural world, as well as an extensive knowledge of the medical history of the Celtic people. It is known that the druids committed all of their incredible knowledge to memory. I see this as a means to hold their sacred power and keep it intact and pure. The ancient druids were a mysterious people. They guarded their secrets and set themselves apart, even as they served the Celtic community as a whole. A great thing about the Irish is they are perfectly okay with not having the answers to everything. They are fine with admitting they don't know. There is an inherent humility and wisdom in that. In fact, when you visit Newgrange, the tour guide will tell you right from the start that no one knows for sure who the ancient people were that built it. And it's true. No one does know for certain, including me. And yet, I have spent decades extensively exploring, learning and contemplating the fascinating and complex history, customs and ways of the druids, ancient Celts and the Irish. And through the prism of those experiences and the lens of my own Celtic lineage, I have come to see that there are patterns, nuances, parallels and synchronicities that emerge and reveal themselves time and time again. I will never claim to know for certain. A bit of mystery has always been okay with me. But when you look at something long enough, sometimes you find that the answers have been right in front of you the whole time. And so it is that I humbly submit that the ancient people who built Newgrange, Knowth, Dowth and Stonehenge over 5,000 years ago are indelibly connected to the Celtic druids through either an ancestral or spiritual lineage, or both. I say that because the connections between the two have been staring us in the face for centuries; the sacred alignment with the cosmos, the stone circles, the mysterious knowledge of the physics of the natural world, and symbols like the triskelion (triple spiral), all of which were known and used by both. And the similarities don't end there. In 1984 the remarkably preserved body of a 2,000 year old druid was unearthed from a peat bog by commercial peat cutters at Lindow Moss in Cheshire, North West England. One of the reasons it was understood to be a druid was that the hands of the man were completely unblemished, with no scars or calluses. For it is said that, where members of all other Celtic societal groups used their hands for countless tasks and activities, the mysterious druids were known to almost exclusively use their minds; an interesting trait that inextricably ties them to the ancients of Newgrange and Stonehenge. Also, although archaeologists indicate that Stonehenge (like Newgrange) was built by a people who predate the Celtic druids; once again there are mysterious ties that bind the two together. For example, it is known that Stonehenge is an ancient astronomical wonder that utilized a 19 year cycle to synchronize lunar and solar years. In 1897 a 2,000 year old Celtic druidic calendar that is considered a masterpiece of calendrical calculation was discovered in France. It uses the exact same 19 year cycle. As I see it, the evidence of the connection between the druids and the ancients who built Stonehenge and Newgrange is undeniable. It is not evidence of the physical sort that archaeologists normally seek, but of the intangible, sacred synchronicities that vibrate with an ancient knowledge that bind the two as one. As I said in the first chapter, I have never believed that the giant stones of Newgrange and Stonehenge were placed there by physical means alone. However those heavy stones were lifted to where they stand today, I believe it involved more of the power of the mind than the strength of the hands. The ancient druids vanished from the earth over 1,500 years ago, but their powerful knowledge and wisdom still whispers to us from the other side of the stones they left behind. That druidic voice beckons us to return to oneness with the earth and stars, and to once again tap into our long lost ability to use our mind to do the heavy lifting of our times.

It was said that he could talk to the Thunder Beings. I once heard a story about Lakota holy man Frank Fools Crow that illustrated a great power of connection to the natural world. As it was told to me, there was an outdoor weekend event of some kind happening on the Pine Ridge Indian reservation in South Dakota back in the 1960s. As morning slipped into afternoon, the skies kept getting darker, and soon a few drops of rain began to spit here and there, threatening to ruin the festivities. It was when the sprinkles began that someone approached Grandpa Frank and asked if there was a prayer he could say to stop the rain. Fools Crow nodded quietly and rose from his chair, got his pipe, fetched his eagle bonnet from the back of his truck and proceeded to make his way toward a nearby hill. When he got there he began to climb up and soon disappeared from sight. After some time, Grandpa Frank reappeared near the bottom of the hill and casually walked back to his truck, tucking away his pipe and bonnet and retaking his seat without saying a word. As the story goes, the dark clouds overhead began to disperse as soon as Fools Crow had returned. The rain stopped and the clouds dissipated until the sun appeared and remained for the rest of the weekend. No one knows what Grandpa Frank Fools Crow did up on the hill that day, but whatever it was, it invoked a great power that had a direct affect on the natural world. As with the Celtic druids, Indigenous medicine people had a mysterious ceremonial access to sacred power that could create movement in the physical realm. I believe it was that same power that both Sitting Bull and Crazy Horse relied on to prevent a bluecoat soldier's bullet from ever striking either of them. There once existed a symbiosis of natural and unseen energy in the ancient Indigenous and Celtic worlds that was akin to being enveloped by the rushing waters of a river. Sadly, we have lost contact with that powerful sacred current today, but the ancient ones were swimming in it.

Distinguished among the Celtic druids were the healers that doctored their people with plant medicine, incantations, prayers and fairy charms. They were revered by Celtic society, and given a place of honor at the royal table beside the nobles. The druidic knowledge of medicinal herbs, roots and poisons was vast, and there are numerous accounts of their treatment methods for every ailment imaginable. Similarly, Indigenous medicine people were also held in great esteem by their communities, and were every bit as important as the headmen, storytellers or clan mothers. Furthermore, they too utilized sacred prayer songs, and possessed an extensive knowledge and intimate spiritual relationship with what they called the plant people. In the previous chapter, I mentioned Indigenous people knowing of a sacred spring in Eureka Springs, Arkansas that once possessed the power to heal blindness. Incidentally, in ancient Ireland, the druids would direct people with ophthalmic issues to the holy wells, as they understood that those sacred waters held the power to cure the eyes and even give sight to the blind. Included in the administering of druidic medicine was the use of sacred numbers; a blessing said 3 times; an incantation recited 3 times, 3 drops of a potion infused, 3 green stones gathered, 9 handfuls of moss dried, 9 pinches of powder applied, 9 shoots of root from the ash tree added, and so on. There are mystical reasons for the use of these sacred numbers in the administering of medicine that are tied to the ancients who left their marks on the stones of Brú na Bóinne (Newgrange) and the like. They too, worked in sacred numerals. I have taken notice that the symbols and markings carved into the stones of these ancient places are all divisible of 3, 4, 7 and 9. And thus, we see yet another mysterious connection that binds the two together. Both the Celtic druids and Indigenous medicine people of ancient times conducted highly complex, elaborate spiritual ceremonies that incorporated the circle, sacred plants, prayer songs, celestial cycles and a deep connection to the earth and the cosmos. Certainly the finer details of the rites differed greatly between the two cultures, but all of those elements mentioned above were central to the ceremonial practices of both.

As I have learned it from the Indigenous cultures I am connected to, there are primarily two types of pouches Native medicine people create and use; the medicine bag and the prayer bag. The former is used to hold herbs that are needed for various purposes. The latter is usually created for someone. The maker will place special, sacred items inside the prayer bag that are infused with prayers for the intended recipient. Once the bag is given, the new owner keeps the bag in a place of honor and never opens it to look inside, for to do so would be disrespectful and the prayer bag would lose its sacred power. Many years ago I was gifted one of these prayer bags. That special gift has been part of my cherished traditional buckskin regalia ever since. Similarly, in one particular druidic remedy, a small bag with a few items inside is given to a person who is suffering with a fever. The bag is worn around the neck, and the wearer must never open it and look at the contents or the charm will be broken. Once again, the synchronicities are clear, as this understanding of mystery is another thread that weaves Indigenous medicine people and the Celtic druids together. Native people have always known that mystery holds power, and that not everything in the world needs to be revealed. Some things are best left hidden from view. Likewise, as I shared previously, the Irish are perfectly okay with not having to know the answers to everything. That trait is undoubtedly a vestige of their ancestral Celtic past. Thus, though culturally unique in their ways and customs, the similarities between Indigenous medicine people and Celtic druidic healers abound. Their shared knowledge of the plants, use of prayer and incantations, reverence for mystery, and understanding of the healing power of sacred waters all speak to an unexplainable, yet undeniable, interwoven spiritual synchronicity between these two ancient peoples.

These strange mystical beings are both feared and revered around the world. Nearly every culture on the planet has old stories about them. They are neither good nor evil, and so can either bring blessings or stir up trouble. They are the fairies, or little people, and their hidden, secret ways have often intersected with great affect into the lives of Indigenous and Celtic people....

I was riding shotgun in my Cherokee friend Leroy's truck when he said it. It was just in passing in the context of a conversation, but he had mentioned the Little People. I chuckled a bit, but Leroy wasn't joking. What he told me next was one of my first excursions into the world of the Little People as Indigenous people know them. Leroy responded to my light chuckle by kindly telling me that I shouldn't laugh. He explained that the Little People were very, very real, and that to laugh at them was not a good idea. He told me the Little People had been known by the Cherokee for centuries. They were the spirit helpers of the medicine people, teaching them the powers of the plants and herbs, and they would do good things for those who showed them respect. Leroy explained that the Little People would sometimes appear in your peripheral vision, but that you should never look directly at them as they would disappear and bad luck would follow. I have since heard many other stories about the Little People since that day in Leroy's truck. The Yankton Sioux told Meriwether Lewis in 1804 of the Little People who lived in Spirit Mound, retelling the story of a terrible encounter with them that left the Yankton people so terrified of them that they would not go near the mound. The Crow people have an old history of interactions with the Little People, saying that they lived in the Pryor Mountains of Montana. The Crow say that the ancient rock carvings in those mountains were made by the Little People. Every year the Crow would make offerings to them at a place they called Medicine Rocks. Though greatly feared, they were also known to impart spiritual wisdom to some people. One such person was a man named Plenty Coups, who had a vision in which the leader of the Little People came to him, took him underground and warned him that the white man would soon be as numerous as the buffalo, and that the Crow would only survive if they listened and learned. And that if they did, their future generations would remain in the land that could be seen from the Medicine Rocks. Guided by the powerful vision Plenty Coups had with the Little People, the Crow did indeed survive, and today their reservation is near the Medicine Rocks, just as his vision foretold. There are Indigenous nations across the Americas that have stories of the Little People. And as I learned from my Cherokee friend Leroy all those years ago, they are very, very real.

In the Celtic world, the fairies were called 'Sidhe', or spirit race, and they existed in an otherworldly place halfway between celestial, angelic beings and humanity. Their ability to slip in and out of the three dimensional world was the power that kept them invisible when they wished to remain hidden. In Celtic understanding, that dimension where the fairy race lives is a place of perpetual youth, beauty and joy. That mystical place is called Tír na nÓg, and some claim to have seen it, having been enchanted by a beautiful fairy maiden. It is said that time moves at a rapid pace in the dimension of Tír na nÓg, as a human being who entered and stayed for a few hours would return to their own realm to find that decades had passed. The fairy-house was called the Sifra, and its entrance could be unveiled by walking around a fairy rath (a circular earthwork) 9 times during a full moon. When the fairies revealed themselves to the ancient Celts it was either to impart a blessing of some kind, or to enlist the help of a human being for something. It was known to be very dangerous to insult a fairy, as they could bring a wrath down on a person that could utterly destroy their life. The fairy healers were usually old women who possessed mysterious, mystical power and a profound knowledge of sacred plants and herbs. Throughout the ages, the fairy race has interacted with the Celtic people, always with their own self interests at heart. For the role of the fairies is not to serve human beings, but rather to act as intermediaries between the celestial and human dimensions. Old Irish custom advises against actively seeking out interactions with the fairies, but to show them respect if they choose to interact with you. Surely there are differing views on the existence of the fairy race, but as they say, the existence of something does not depend on whether it is believed or not. Again, seeing is not a requirement for something to be real. As with the overwhelming evidence of connections I observed between the druids and the ancients, I once again find that the answer to questions about the fairies is hiding in plain sight. The existence of these mystical beings has been acknowledged by human beings from around the world for thousands of years. Those who only trust in the three dimensions, convinced that a given thing must belong in that world to be real, can find that the realities of other dimensional worlds are concealed from their view. It is only when we allow our paradigms to expand and open ourselves to see the un-seeable that the impossible becomes possible.

Once again, we see the mysterious synchronicities of two unique peoples, oceans apart, yet somehow joined together in sacred alignment. The ways of both druidic healers and Indigenous medicine people were infused with the ancient humming energy of the unseen world. Their shared ability to affect the physics of the natural world, extensive knowledge of medicinal plants, use of sacred incantations, and interactions with a race of mysterious beings from a parallel dimension all speak to an unexplainable common source. The ancient Celts and Indigenous people are as two branches from the same tree. They may each reach for the sun and waters in their own way, but both are anchored to the same ancient life force that indelibly ties them together with roots that wind and twist deep into the mysteries of the earth. That sacred power is the unseen cosmic web, that fires with the unimaginable energy, that the ancients knew how to access and harness for everything from moving a giant stone to healing a broken body. For too long we have wandered in the darkness, lost and disconnected from the celestial cycles and synchronistic rhythms that still call to our spirits like an echo from a forgotten time. Humanity has become separated from mysticism, unable to see beyond the veil or hear the still, small voice of the sacred. The secret messages of astronomical alignment with the cosmos whisper to us from beyond the stars, and beckon us to step back into the unknown, that we may know ourselves once again and return to the place of oneness in the ancient, sacred circle *of mist and stone.*

I am an estuary into the sea.

I am a wave of the ocean.

I am the sound of the sea.

I am a powerful ox.

I am a hawk on a cliff.

I am a dewdrop in the sun.

I am a plant of beauty.

I am a boar for valour.

I am a salmon in a pool.

I am a lake in a plain.

I am the strength of art.

Amhairghin

CIRCLING BACK
~ IN SUMMATION – FINDING THE MISSING NOTE ~

As I've toured throughout the states over the decades, I cannot count how many times I have heard it, people at my meet and greet table at an event telling me that they are Native and Irish. It has happened nearly everywhere we have ever been. The reason for this phenomenon should be made clear by this book. When the Irish came to America, they experienced a continuation of the oppression they had suffered for centuries in their homeland, so they could empathize with Native people. Also, the Irish are the descendants of the Celts, who saw the earth as the mother, had a circular worldview and ascribed to a system of honor. So it makes sense that so many Irish would find Native people and their ways appealing. In chapter 4 I told the story of how the Irish helped the Cherokee during the ethnic cleansing period of forced removal (a.k.a. the 'Trail of Tears'), even taking Cherokee babies into their homes to care for them. Well, as it turns out, the Cherokee and Irish ended up making a lot of babies together! It seems that everywhere the Irish went in America they intermarried with Native people along the way. Even in Canada, though not near as much as the French, Irish bloodlines are part of Métis Indigenous genetic background, and some Irish customs have been melded into Métis traditions. In short, Native-Irish people are everywhere. In fact, I'm one of them. Amid all the oral history of Indigenous heritage that was imparted to me when I was young, there were also mentions of Irish lineage, though not as often. It wouldn't be until many decades later that my Irish Celtic ancestors would finally come alive in me and become a meaningful part of the fabric of my identity through a fascinating series of synchronistic events.

Brother Seamus Byrne is a monastic and a musician from Wicklow, Ireland who was attending a Catholic music retreat in Eureka Springs, Arkansas back in 2001. Seamus composes and performs enchanting, Celtic music using an assortment of instruments, including Irish flutes and whistles, a traditional Irish drum called the bodhran and his lovely voice. He also owns a small Native American cedar flute, and loves to perform with that as part of his repertoire. One evening at the retreat, Seamus gave a performance of his music, which included a song on his Native flute. Afterward, a woman approached Seamus and mentioned that the song he had played on that flute had reminded her of my music. Seamus responded by asking if there was any way he might be able to meet me, and she put him in touch with Carley Perry, Peggy's mom. On that same night, we had made plans for a dinner at our place with some friends. The meal was cooked and ready when our friends called and apologized for having to suddenly cancel. Before we could decide what to do with all the food, the phone rang again. This time it was Peggy's mom, Carley. She explained that she had a visitor who was a monastic musician from Ireland who wanted to meet me, and asked if she could bring him by for a visit. So we had a new friend over for dinner that night, Brother Seamus Byrne.

There are people you meet in this life that you have an instant bond with. Seamus is one of those people for me and Peggy. From the moment we met that first night, it felt like we were old friends. And it was during that visit that something synchronistic was revealed. Seamus got out his instruments, which of course included the Native flute that had played such a role in our meeting. When I saw the flute, I was immediately struck by its design. It looked familiar to me. In fact, it looked like it had been made by the same man who had made one of my favorite flutes, but I thought that was inconceivable. How could that be? My flute had been gifted to me in Arkansas and Seamus had bought his in California. So I fetched my flute and we began to look them over. The maker of my flute was an Osage man named Nev. He didn't make a lot of flutes, as there was a lot of handcrafting involved with his design, but the flutes he did make were awesome and highly sought after. As we examined our two instruments, I remembered that I knew a secret about Nev's flutes. He was a humble man and didn't like the idea of putting his name on his instruments where it could be seen. So he would just print 'Nev' in pencil on the inside of the hole at the end of the flute. When we shined a light into the end of Seamus' flute, lo and behold, there it was, the name 'Nev' in pencil, just like mine. What are the odds that an Irish monk from Ireland would not only have a Native flute, but one made by the same maker that made mine? And what are the odds that he would travel to an ancient mountain in Arkansas, play that flute and have its song lead him to me? What are the odds? Astronomical.

It wasn't long before Seamus and I were working on an album together. It was called *Traditions*, and joined Celtic and American Indian music styles together. One particular song on the album was called *Ancient Forests*, and featured my 'Nev' Native flute and Seamus' boxwood Celtic flute. When we recorded the song, we discovered that in order to play our two flutes in harmony, there was one note on each that could not be played. So, I avoided that note on mine, and Seamus avoided it on his. As we toured with the album, that story about avoiding a note in order to achieve harmony became a parable. The message was that, when we wish to be in harmony with someone different from us, we should be willing to sacrifice a note; and that doing so is an act of grace that creates the music of friendship and understanding. Over many months of touring, Seamus and I shared that message with the audiences we performed for. Then, one night at a concert at the historic Opera House in Grand Ledge, Michigan, something remarkable happened. I was in the middle of sharing the story of the missing note when Seamus leaned into his mic and said, "John, I have a confession to make." I replied, "What is it Seamus?" And he responded with a grin, "I've been playing the note." The audience roared. When the laughter subsided, I said to Seamus, "I too, have a confession to make." He said with a smile, "Yes, John?" To which I replied, "So have I." Again the audience erupted in laughter. Seamus and I went on that night to share a fascinating experience we had both had with our forbidden notes. We had discovered that, the more we performed the song together, the places where each of our 'disharmonious notes' could be played were revealed to us. And a profound lesson emerged. We find harmony when we learn to walk in each other's shoes. At the start, we harmonize what we can, and save the sour notes for later. And once we truly know and understand one another, we can even find a way to include those sour notes in the song of our compassion, empathy and friendship. Meeting Seamus was a life changing moment of synchronicity for me. His friendship awakened the dormant voice of my Irish ancestors, opened my ears to hear their hidden stories and led me back to the homeland from which they came. I am deeply grateful for my friend Seamus. Without him, this book would have never been written. I am grateful for his open heart, his gentleness, his knowledge and his kindness. And I am grateful that he too, heard the whisper of the ancient synchronicity and oneness that Celtic and Indigenous people share. After all, why else would an Irish monk be drawn to give a voice to a Native American flute?

From the time I was a small boy, I have sought out the quiet spaces and spent time in them, contemplating, reflecting and seeking to understand. History has always weighed heavy on my heart, and in some strange, mysterious way it has always been alive, breathing and real to me. I have always felt a deep bond with historic and ancient people and places, and reached out to touch them, to know them and feel them. During a visit to Monticello, the historic home of the 3rd President of the United States, Thomas Jefferson, I stood in his slave quarters and felt myself nearly slip through the veil of time. I could feel them they were so close. I whispered a few quiet words of lament and compassion to them, and then slipped back to my own present time. I have also stood at the desk in Montpelier where James Madison looked out the window over his expansive property and penned the words to the U.S. Constitution. I could almost see him sitting there, shaping the future of a new nation. It was the same when I visited the cottage of Irish patriot Pádraic Pearse. Whenever I stand in the places where history is still touchable, I can't help but slip through that veil and feel it as it was. For me, those people and places are not gone. Time does not separate them from me. When I can touch what they touched, see what they saw and feel what they felt, then the time between us is erased and I find myself present in their world if even just for a fleeting moment. With my hand resting gently on an ancient stone carving at Newgrange, 5,200 years suddenly vanished and became as thin as a veil, through which I could glimpse the forgotten world of an unknown people on the other side of the mist.

I wrote this book because, as I look around at the world we live in today, with all our technological advancements, I see something slipping away – our reverence for the sacred, ancient mysteries. With our bustling cities, high rise lifestyles and flat-screen fixations, we are adrift. When you stand at a place like Newgrange, and see the monumental effort that went into honoring the sacred by a people we can't even remember, it becomes apparent that somehow, over the millennia, our priorities have gotten mixed up. As I see humanity struggling to make sense of life, and straining to find meaning in the meaningless, my spirit is drawn back to the ancient places and people who held the answers we seek today. I want you to know that they were real, and that time doesn't have to separate us from what they knew. We can touch it again. We can find our way back to the sacred stones, and reconnect. The ancient messages they left behind are still with us, in us. We need only to look beyond the glimmer of the artificial and fix our gaze on the deep substance of what is real. For the answers lie not in the temporal things which dazzle for a moment and then slip away and turn to dust, they lie in the sacred power of the infinite – the circle, the cycles and the center. For too long there has been a missing note in our world. The ancients knew that note. Let us lean in to hear it once again, that we may circle back and find our way.

EXPLORING FURTHER

~ SUGGESTED BOOKS, MUSIC, FILMS AND PLACES ~

It is my intention that this book will serve as a portal into a nearly forgotten time through which the reader can travel and begin to rediscover ancient truths and sacred meaning for life. And it is my hope that it will be as the seed of a sacred oak, planted in the soil of the heart, to then grow and reach for more connection, understanding and expansion. In that spirit, I would like to suggest the following books to read, films to see, music to listen to and places to visit. All of the following have contributed to writing of this book.

Suggested Reading:
The Long March by Marie-Louise Fitzpatrick

Malachy McCourt's History of Ireland by Malachy McCourt

Bury My Heart at Wounded Knee by Dee Brown

Thirteen Moons on Turtle's Back by Joseph Bruchac

White Birch, Red Hawthorn – A Memoir - by Nora Murphy

Claiming Breath by Diane Glancy

How the Irish Saved Civilization by Thomas Cahill

Black Elk Speaks by John G. Neihardt

Who Were the Celts by Kevin Duffy

Neither Wolf Nor Dog by Kent Nerburn

The Girl Who Sang to the Buffalo by Kent Nerburn

Last Words by Piaras F. Mac Lochlainn

Lame Deer, Seeker of Visions by John (Fire) Lame Deer and Richard Erdoes

The Spirit of the Celtic Gods and Goddesses by Carl McColman and Kathryn Hinds

Mother Earth Spirituality by Ed McGaa, Eagle Man

Irish Cures, Mystic Charms & Superstitions by Lady Wilde, compiled by Sheila Anne Barry

Flutes in the Garden by Chip Richards

Suggested Films:
Bury My Heart at Wounded Knee (features my music!)

Black '47

The New World

Michael Collins

Smoke Signals

<u>Suggested Music</u>:
Of Mist and Stone – John Two-Hawks
(the music that goes with this book!)

Prayer Songs and Symphonic Poems – Manach (Brother Seamus Byrne)

Traditions – Indian-Celtic Music & Spirit –
John Two-Hawks & Manach (Brother Seamus Byrne)

Watermark – Enya

Outlander, Original Television Series Soundtrack Volume I –
Bear McCreary

Beautiful World – John Two-Hawks

A New Journey – Celtic Woman

Healing Flute Music for Calm and Inspiration – Brother Seamus Byrne

Idjagieđas – In the Hand of the Night – Mari Boine

Horse Spirit – John Two-Hawks

<u>Suggested Places to Visit</u>:
Medicine Wheel, Wyoming USA

Newgrange, Donore, Co Meath, Ireland

Knowth & Dowth, Drogheda, Co Meath, Ireland

Mato Tipi ('Devil's Tower'), Wyoming USA

Sedona, Arizona USA

Pádraic Pearse Cottage and Cultural Centre, Inbhear, near Ros Muc, Co Galway, Ireland

Wounded Knee Mass Grave, Wounded Knee, Pine Ridge Indian Reservation, South Dakota USA

Famine Mass Grave, Kinvara, Ireland

The Aran Islands, Galway Bay, Ireland

Wind Cave National Park, South Dakota USA

Brigit's Garden, Pollagh, Rosscahill, Co Galway, Ireland

The Black Hills, South Dakota USA

The Ring of Kerry, Iveragh Peninsula, Co Kerry, Ireland

Cliffs of Moher, Co Clare, Ireland

Dingle Peninsula, South-West Ireland

An Buntsop Cottage, Galway, Ireland

Servants of Love Monastic Community, Wicklow, Ireland

Eureka Springs, Arkansas USA

Brownshill Dolmen, Carlow, Ireland
(the largest dolmen in Ireland)

Poulnabrone Dolmen, The Burren, Co Clare, Ireland

Lastly, any visit to Ireland must include visits to the ancient castles, churches and abbeys which can be found anywhere near where you happen to be, there are so many of them. And be sure to look for those stone circles and spend some time connecting.

John Two-Hawks is a Grammy® nominated recording artist and author of numerous books on spirituality, culture and personal healing. A mixed blood person of Lakota and Irish descent, John's music, books and talks impart earth-based approaches to physical, emotional and spiritual health and wellness, and inspire people to live a balanced life of purpose and passion.

For in-person events and online talks and courses on this book and more, and to get the audio book, e-book and music, visit johntwohawks.com

Teresa Sullivan is a gifted artist who specializes in acrylic and oil painting as well as nature photography. She strives to inspire others to see the joy in the world around them with her beautiful art. Teresa's paintings evoke feeling and tell a story that resonates with meaning.

spiritedartstms@yahoo.com